A Boomer's Guide to Long-term Care

A Boomer's Guide to Long-term Care

2006 E-Published

Published by e-FinancialWriter.com,, Jupiter, FL 33478, U.S.A.
©2006 e-FinancialWriter.com. All rights reserved. No part of this
publication may be reproduced, stored in a retrieval system, or
transmitted in any form or by any means, electronic, mechanical,
recording or otherwise, without the prior written permission of e-
FinancialWriter.com.

Manufactured in the United States of America.

ISBN-13 978-1-60145-094-4
ISBN-10 1-60145-094-X

Booklocker.com, Inc.
2006

A Boomer's Guide to Long-term Care

George D. Lambert, III

A Boomer's Guide to Long-term Care

INTRODUCTION

The author does not sell insurance or have links on his Website advertising insurance companies. However, he has seen how the skyrocketing costs of long-term care expenses can wreck a family's finances. And he wanted to offer the benefit of his experience so it doesn't happen to you.

TABLE OF CONTENTS

AUTHOR'S BACKGROUND

George D. Lambert III is a freelance financial writer; and an NASD and a NYSE Arbitrator. He has been a Certified Financial Planner™ and a Certified Divorce Financial Analyst, and has held numerous securities and insurance licenses.

During his financial planning career, George designed and presented seminars on retirement planning, pre-divorce financial planning for women, and planned giving.

George earned a Bachelor of Business Administration Degree (summa cum laude) from Northwood University, West Palm Beach, Florida and lives in Jupiter, Florida with his wife, Linda, and son, Corey.

For information on George's services, visit
http://e-FinancialWriter.com

or e-mail him at:
GDLambert@e-financialwriter.com

DISCLAIMER

This book is designed to provide accurate and authoritative information in regard to the subject matter covered. It is made available with the understanding that the publisher and author are not rendering legal, accounting or other professional service. Legal advice and other expert assistance should be obtained prior to implementing any technique discussed in this book.

A SCARY THOUGHT

Getting old is scary. The oldest boomers turned 60 in 2006, yet many of us are in a state of denial when it comes to aging. But what's the alternative? And when it comes to possibly needing long-term care (LTC), well that's not gonna to happen to me.

Nevertheless, this is the biggest financial risk many of us face. And most of us are not prepared.

We worry about protecting our lives, incomes, homes, cars, boats, and possessions from financial loss. Yet too many of us don't have any plans on how to cover the biggest risk we face.

Do you think this is a problem that doesn't affect the wealthy? Well, think again.

Northern Trust conducted a survey of households with $1 million or more of investable assets. They found that the participants believed rapidly rising health care cost was the number one potential obstacle to enjoying retirement.[1]

There are boomers who will retire in their early 60s. And with life expectancies ever rising, there's a good chance that you'll live into your 80s, 90s, or longer after you retire.

So what can you do to make sure a sickness or injury over the next 20 or 30 years doesn't leave you, your spouse, or your heirs with nothing but bills?

One option, of course, is to simply stick your head in the sand and keep telling yourself that getting sick and needing help only happens to the other guy.

COMPLICATED ISSUE

Long-term care is a complicated issue, in which there is a lack of knowledge. A 2006 survey sponsored by John Hancock Life Insurance Company included a 10-question true/false quiz about LTC basics.[2] The majority of respondents got only four answers correct.

This book is not intended to make you an expert. You need to know, though, what questions to ask. It doesn't matter whether you're talking to a caseworker at Medicare or an insurance agent. If you don't know what to ask or don't understand the basic terms, you'll be at a distinct disadvantage.

The costs

According to the 2005 MetLife Mature Market Institute studies, the nation's average basic rate of long-term care is:

- $64,240 a year for a semi-private nursing home room
- $74,095 a year for a private nursing home room
- $19 per hour for home health aids to provide in-home care

You can find the rates for your community on the Website listed in the Appendix.

And even though some of the prices are more than you'd pay to live in a five-star hotel, they are just averages. You might not want to settle for average care. For example, how do you feel about sharing a bathroom with other residents?

The odds you'll need care

A study noted in *The Wall Street Journal* determined that 69 percent of today's 65-year olds will eventually need long-term care, and 37 percent will need the type of care provided in a nursing home or assisted-living facility.[3]

Nevertheless, long-term care doesn't necessarily mean nursing home care. Many people just require help with custodial tasks, such as getting dressed, bathing, or using the toilet. Family members or friends can easily provide this type of care. But do you have someone you can count on? Depending on your kids can be a dangerous assumption. After all, they have their own lives to live, careers to pursue, and children to chase after.

So if you're lucky, you won't get seriously ill from eating too much fast food all your adult life and not need help tying your shoes or eating your oatmeal.

But suppose you're the kind of guy or gal who has never won a lottery or anything else and generally think of yourself as not very lucky? Here's what you could face at some point during retirement:

- Eleven percent of 65-year men and 28 percent of women will end up needing more than five years of care at home or in a facility
- Eight percent of people getting benefits from a three-year benefit long-term care insurance policy will use up their coverage
- Six percent of those entering a nursing home as a private payer will end up on Medicaid

Still not convinced?

A report published by Genworth Financial noted that Alzheimer's disease is one of the fastest growing diseases in the U.S.[4] And it accounted for 40% of every dollar of claims paid to long-term care providers. There are an estimated 4.5 million Alzheimer's sufferers—double what was in 1980. This number could hit 7.7 million by the year 2030.

The report's authors went on to state that 70 percent of single people and 50 percent of married couples who require long-term care become destitute. Furthermore, caring for Alzheimer's patients will put tremendous demographic and financial pressures on the country as the baby boomers age.

So how much of your net worth are you willing to give up to pay for this care? Assume that the average value of a home in U.S. is $230,000. With long-term care averaging $74,000 per year, selling your home should buy you a little over three years worth of care.

A WOMAN IS AT GREATER RISK

Women have a bigger problem than men because statistically they live longer. Consider this example: A woman cares for her increasingly frail husband; he dies. Then she needs special care, there is no one to help, and she must go to a nursing home.

Spend some time in a nursing home. You'll come out with this conclusion: The majority of long-term nursing home residents tend to be single, female, over age 80, and suffering from dementia. They don't have any family support and are unable to live independently.

YOUR CHOICES

SELF INSURE

Before you take this route, consider two things: future income and what you own.

When projecting your income in retirement, will you include Social Security? Considering the state of the federal budget and the talk by the people in Washington about slicing benefits (But I imagine not for them) many boomers aren't counting much on Social Security.

Will your income depend on interest from CDs and savings accounts? An interest rate drop could mean less income to cover your living needs, including long-term care costs. Lower interest rates could also affect bonds since the issuers might call in the bonds and force you to reinvest elsewhere at lower rates.

Or maybe you're counting on real estate or stocks to support yourself in retirement. That's wonderful. Except what will happen if your expenses shoot up by $5,000 or $6,000 a month because of long-term care costs? You'll be forced to sell something. And it just might be a lousy time in the market. Plus what'll happen after you've recovered? The real estate or stock is gone, and so is a source of your income.

The Bureau of Labor Statistics found in its 2001 Survey of Consumer Finances that the average household with heads aged 70 years or younger and not retired has $101,518.85 in financial assets.[5] Therefore, if that describes you and you needed long-term care, you would go through all of your money in less than two years.

7

What is your check-writing tolerance level? With average stays of 2 ½ years at $74,000 per year, how would you feel writing a check for $185,000? Or what if you and your spouse needed care? $370,000 is a big number for most people. They're just averages, too. Can you write that big of a check without your hand shaking?

Suppose, though, that you've worked out the numbers and figured that you have enough set aside to cover two or three years' of the extra expenses. Terrific. But wait. This could be money that will not go to your love ones or favorite charity. Are you willing to shortchange them?

RELY ON FAMILY AND FRIENDS

A generation ago this was the norm. Perhaps your parents lived close to your grandparents when you were a kid. Then when one grandparent died, the survivor might have moved in with you and your parents. And maybe you have or are helping your parents or in-laws. With each generation, though, this is becoming more and more difficult—and stressful.

According to an Urban Institute's report[6]:

- About three-quarters of frail, older people receiving assistance outside of a nursing home rely on unpaid caregivers.
- Unpaid caregivers provide an average of 201 hours per month to help with personal activities and household chores.
- Nine out of ten married, frail Americans receive help from their spouse. One out of three of the caregiver-spouses have health problems themselves.
- More than half who need assistance are unmarried and receive help from their daughters.
- More than half of adult children helping their frail parents are employed.

This can obviously be a significant burden on those who do their best to provide the needed care as they try to balance personal responsibilities with work demands. These caregivers may feel isolated from their friends and overwhelmed by their responsibilities. The result can be high stress levels, depression, and physical ailments.

Even if they're willing to help, could they do it fulltime? Not likely. You might still need someone to come in a few hours a day. For example, if you required a home health aid four hours at day during the week at $19 per hour, the cost would be $380 a week. Six months of this could run $9,880.00.

A problem for the recipient, however, may be that the care they get might not be sufficient or proper. Plus the caregivers might not be immediately available when an emergency pops up, especially in the middle of the night.

As the population ages, there could be a shortfall in the number of available unpaid caregivers. This problem could further compound because of:

- Rising divorce rates
- Declining family sizes
- Relocations
- More women working outside the home

Bottom line—If you have any friends or family who you think would be able to provide proper care and willing to put up with you when you're old, sick, and cranky, this is the way to go.

RELY ON THE GOVERNMENT

There are two main sources of government assistance. Medicare pays if you are medically-needy, and Medicaid pays if you are financially-needy.

MEDICARE

Generally you won't be eligible for Medicare until you reach 65. But before we go any further, let's discuss the three main levels of long-term care:

- **Skilled Care:** 24-hour-a-day prescribed care provided by licensed medical professionals who are under the direct supervision of a physician. Medicare *will* pay for a limited amount of this level of care. You must, however, meet certain conditions.
- **Intermediate Care:** Prescribed care that can be provided on an intermittent, rather than continuous basis - for example, physical therapy.
- **Custodial Care:** Care that assists people with daily living requirements, such as dressing, eating and personal hygiene. This is what most people need when they get sick or hurt and includes Alzheimer's disease patients.

Medicare will only pay for skilled care after you have been in the hospital for at least three days. And you must enter a Medicare-approved nursing home within 30 days of leaving the hospital. It will pay for the care for up to 100 days as long as you continue to meet the requirements. Plus there are deductibles along the way. After 100 days, you're on your own—no matter what's wrong with you.

How patients and Medicare pay for skilled nursing home care (2006 rates)[7]

Number of Days	Patients Pay	Medicare Pays
Days 1-20	Nothing	Everything
Days 21-100	$119.00 per day	The balance
Over 100 days	Everything	Nothing

If you need care in a skilled nursing home at a later time, you must meet the same conditions again for Medicare to pay.

Your doctor must have ordered daily, skilled care. There are more hoops that Medicare will make you and your doctor jump through to get any of their money. You can read about them on Medicare's Website listed in the Appendix.

Bottom line—You must be in pretty bad shape to get Medicare's limited, short-term help with your long-term care expense. Don't count on it.

MEDICAID

Medicaid is the federal-state program that covers health care for the poor and is the nation's chief source of funding for two-thirds of nursing home residents.[8] You must meet strict income and asset rules to qualify.

Per federal guidelines your spouse can keep the homestead (as long as he or she lives in it) and $99,540 worth of jointly-owned assets. But the states can drop this number all the way down to $19,908. Also your spouse can keep his or her income and no more than $1,603.75 to $2,488.50 per month of your income depending on your state's guidelines.

Following is a hypothetical example of how this could work for a married couple when one of them requires long-term care.

Asset	Value	Countable
House	$ 250,000	
Vacation home	$ 100,000	$ 100,000
Mutual funds	$ 75,000	$ 75,000
401(k)	$ 50,000	$ 50,000
Annuities	$ 100,000	$ 100,000
Stocks	$ 50,000	$ 50,000
Total	$ 625,000	$ 375,000
Less max. exclusion		$ (99,540)
Total exposed		$ 275,460

In this case, the couple must spend $275,460 of their assets before one of them could qualify for Medicaid.

If you are single, the situation is worse yet. Generally you will be eligible for Medicaid after you have only $2,000 of cash and investments left—in other words—when you're just about broke.

Will the government loosen up the purse strings? Consider this and then decide:

A 2005 analysis of the nation's Medicaid program found that states are under-funding the actual cost of providing seniors' nursing home care by at least $4.5 billion annually. And Medicaid payment rates continue to fall dangerously far behind the actual cost of providing quality patient care.[5]

You can read more about the federal guidelines at Medicaid's Website listed in the Appendix.

Bottom line—

- The cost of care continues to rise
- The amount of government payments continues to decline
- The quality of care could suffer
- You must be almost broke to get Medicaid

Don't count on it.

Medicaid planning – There are ways to transfer assets from your name in order to eventually qualify for Medicaid.

And being the benevolent souls they are, the government does not count your car or home in the figure. Don't, however, think that you could sell all your investments then dump everything into your house. The boys (and gals) in Washington are slick to that one (probably because they've done it themselves).

A 2006 revision to the rules disqualifies you from receiving Medicaid if you have home equity of more than $500,000 (states can increase this to $750,000). Furthermore, within the same revision it became harder to qualify for Medicaid by giving away your assets. The government can consider anything that you gave away over the prior five years as countable assets. Previously, the look-back period was three years.

They still haven't put a cap on how much you could invest in a car, though. So conceivably you could stick your money into one of the world's most expensive cars, the $1.25 million Bugatti Veyron 16.4, and possibly qualify for Medicaid.

If you want to look further into Medicaid planning, a good reference book is listed in the Appendix.

Bottom line—The government has become more concerned that wealthier seniors who have the means to pay for their own care are abusing the system. Therefore, it will become increasingly harder to implement Medicaid planning.

TAP YOUR HOME EQUITY

You're required to pay for care if you are single and your home has equity over $500,000. States can raise this to $750,000. Married couples are still exempt from the ceiling if one spouse lives in the home. But Medicaid can recover the cost of any nursing home care from a forced house sale after both spouses die.

If you are single and your home equity exceeds the ceiling, you could use the equity to pay for care by:

- selling it
- borrowing against the equity
- using a reverse mortgage

A reverse mortgage might also be a good idea if you are married and your spouse needs long-term care.

A reverse mortgage is a non-recourse loan that lets homeowners age 62 and older convert the equity in their house into cash. Yet it allows them to still live there, and retain title and ownership. The lender will give you the payout all at once, as a fixed monthly income (up to lifetime), as a line of credit, or as a combination of these.

The money will have to be paid back with interest when you die, sell the home, or permanently move out. But you or your heirs will have the option to pay off the reverse mortgage at anytime and keep the house. And the amount that must be repaid can never exceed the value of the home. Furthermore, if the sales price exceeds the amount owed, the excess will go to you or your estate.

There is no income or medical requirement to qualify for a reverse mortgage. And you can use the money anyway you wish.

The size of the reverse mortgage depends on several factors, including the youngest homeowner's age, the home's value, and current interest rates. The money you receive will be tax-free and not affect Social Security or Medicare benefits. However, it could influence Medicaid qualification.

You could receive the additional income to spend any way you wish. You'll continue to live in your house while your spouse receives the needed care in a nursing facility or at home.

Take for example, Ozzie and Harriet, ages 64 and 62 respectively. They own their home, which is valued at $250,000. Health problems prevented both from obtaining long-term care insurance. Harriet needed in-home care after falling off a ladder and breaking her leg in two places. They didn't have the money to pay for this type of care. A reverse mortgage offered Ozzie and Harriet the following options:[9]

Single lump sum or line of credit - $119,211

Lifetime monthly income - $732

You can read more about reverse mortgages by visiting the link listed in the Appendix.

AN IRREVOCABLE TRUST

An asset protection trust is another option as long as you and your spouse are relatively healthy and you don't think you'll need care for at least five years. After five years, any funds in the trust would not be included in the Medicaid's eligibility calculations. However, the trust is irrevocable. So neither you nor your spouse could touch the principal, but you could receive income.

Another potential problem is if you require care before the Medicaid five-year lookback period expires, the assets in the trust will be considered transferred assets that will trigger the penalty period.

LONG-TERM CARE INSURANCE (LTCI)

LTCI is a popular subject with many older people. Often this is because they frequently have seen friends or relatives impoverished due to the high cost of long-term care. And you too, might have experienced an aging parent who needed help with daily activities at some point during their lives. Were you or your spouse able to give up an established career with a regular paycheck in order to become their caretaker?

Despite the negative consequences, only 16 percent of men and 14 percent of women, age 50 and older, report having a long-term care insurance policy.[10]

How do you plan to remain independent, preserve your freedom of choice, and protect your assets if your health changes after retirement?

What to look for in a policy

Selecting a LTCI is not easy—it takes work. For even with an agent's help, you must understand the various terms and benefits, and then compare the costs.

Financial stability of company

Only work with companies that have one of the top two credit ratings from at least two of agencies listed in the Appendix. Take note though because the letter signifying the rating may not mean the same thing with each agency. For instance, a "B" from Weiss falls into the "secure-good" category. But an "A" from Moody's or a "BBB" from Fitch or S&P mean the same thing.

	Description	A.M. Best	S&P	Fitch	Moody's	Weiss
Secure	Superior	A++, A+				
	Exceptionally Strong		AAA	AAA	Aaa	
	Excellent	A, A-			Aa	A
	Very Strong		AA	AA		
	Very Good	B++, B+				
	Strong		A	A		
	Good		BBB	BBB	A	B
	Adequate				Baa	
Vulnerable	Fair	B, B-				C
	Questionable				Ba	
	Moderately Weak			BB		
	Marginal	C++, C+	BB			
	Weak	C, C-	B	B		D
	Poor	D			B	
	Very Weak		CCC	CC, CC, C	Caa	E
	Extremely Weak		CC		Ca	
	Failed					F
	Distressed			DDD, DD, D	C	
	Under Regulatory Supervision	E	R			
	In Liquidation	F				
	Suspended	S				
	Unrated		NR			U

Medical exams

Make sure the company wants to check your medical background.

You may wonder why you would not want to go with a company that didn't ask medical questions. After all, you might have a health condition that you believe would be better not discussed. Plus it might be cheaper to go with a company that didn't make you answer a health questionnaire or request doctors' statements.

But in the fine print, there's a good chance that they do their medical investigating *after* you apply for benefits. Then they'll have the option to fight paying claims based on a pre-existing condition clause in the contract.

Historical rate increases

Regardless of your age or health history, companies can't boost long-term care premiums for individual customers. This means that the policy is guaranteed renewable. They can, though, raise rates for a group of policyholders. So take it as a given that there is a real good chance your policy's premiums will go up as time ticks on.

Furthermore, be leery of a quote that is considerably lower than others for a similar plan. It just might be an effort to low-ball you into a policy that will have huge increases in the future.

Ask if the policy includes a rate guarantee. You might find out that there is a three-or-five-year built-in guarantee. Or the company may offer extended guarantees for an additional cost.

Large increases can devastate a retiree's fixed income budget. However, over the recent years insurance companies have gotten a better handle on the actual costs of their policies. Plus state insurance commissioners are making it tougher for insurers to raise rates. Therefore, there is a better chance that future rate increases will be more moderate than they were in the past.

Some states' insurance commissioners, such as California's, publish companies' historical rate increases on their Websites. This data may go back a decade or more and include the:

- Date the policies were sold
- Percentage increase requested
- Percentage increase approved
- Date the rate increase was issued to policy holders

You can find your state commissioner's link by going to the National Association of Insurance Commissioner's Website listed in the Appendix.

Limited pay premiums

Check out policies with single-pay, 10-year, 20-year, and pay-to-65 accelerated payment options. These guarantee that your rate will not increase. Plus if you can pay for a policy over a 10-or-20-year period before you retire, the policy might be paid-up. Therefore, payments won't become a burden once you are on a fixed income during retirement.

Understand, though, that if you stop paying premiums before the payment plan ends, you might not receive any contribution credit, adjustment, or refund for the amount paid.

What qualifies

There are six standard activities of daily living (ADLs) recognized in long-term care policies. These are the basic activities of caring for oneself that you do to live independently.

The ADLs are:

- Eating
- Using the bathroom
- Moving back and forth from a bed to a chair
- Bathing
- Dressing
- Maintaining continent

Look for a policy that will pay when you are unable to perform two or more of the six ADLs. Be aware though, of how a company defines ADLs. For example, a policy might count bathing and dressing as two separate ADLs. Other policies might combine the two into a single ADL. The latter would mean that if you lost the ability to dress *and* bath yourself, you would have to lose a third ADL for the policy benefits to kick in.

There's nothing pleasant about envisioning life without control of these basic functions.
But there is one thing that's worse: needing help with them and not having the money to pay for it.

Facility restrictions

You want a policy that will pay for care in any facility licensed by your state. This includes care for skilled, intermediate, or custodial needs. Be aware that some companies will only pay for care that is supervised by an RN. Others allow supervision by an LPN or licensed vocational nurse, but only under an RN's direction.

Also look for a policy that pays for care in assisted-living facilities. But it might have restrictions. For instance, it may specify that a facility staff member be on the premises 24 hours a day, a doctor be on-call, or the facility be capable of supervising medications.

Waiting period

This is the number of days you must receive care before the policy's benefits begin. Depending on the insurance company, the waiting period options can range from zero to 365 days. The longer the waiting period, the lower the premium. Of course, the longer the waiting period, the more you'll have to pay out of pocket during your initial care. Equate it to the deductible on your auto or homeowners insurance. But that's where the simplicity ends.

Insurance companies can differ in how they define waiting period. They might start counting the days as soon as you are impaired, even if you are in a hospital and not receiving any long-term-care services. Other policies will not begin counting until your qualified long-term-care services begin. And there are some that will only count the days that you receive continuous covered services towards the waiting period.

With this last definition, it could take a long time to use up your waiting period. For example, suppose you receive in-home care three days a week. It could take you over seven months to meet a 90-day waiting period.

You might even be able to find a policy that once the waiting period is satisfied, it will never apply again during your lifetime.

Do some math before you decide. Suppose you needed care that costs $150 per day. With a 90-day waiting period plan, you'd spend $13,500 before the insurance kicks in. A 60-day waiting period would cost you $9,000 out-of-pocket—a $4,500 savings. How much will that difference cost you, though, in higher premiums? Compare.

Daily benefit

This is the maximum per-day amount that the insurance company will pay for qualified expenses. The higher the benefit, the higher your premium. It would be great to insure for whatever the going rate is for long-term care costs in your community. But remember, insurance should be bought to cover the expenses that you can't afford to pay yourself. So be practical.

In 2005, the average rate for a private room in a nursing home was $203 per day. A semi-private costs $176. You can find rates for your area at the link listed in the Appendix. Determine how much of the daily care you could pay on your own. Then insure for the rest. Don't forget that the listed rates do not include drugs, supplies, and special services.

As an example, suppose the care in your area cost $200 per day. A three-year stay would run $219,000. How much of that could you afford to take from your investments while not affecting your lifestyle? Would spending $55,000 make a big difference? If not, you could be comfortable with a policy that paid a $150 per day benefit. However, in case spending the $55,000 would mean not enjoying life after you recover, you better go for a higher daily benefit.

Benefit type

Most likely, the companies you get quotes from will offer reimbursement plans. These pay the actual charges incurred up to the daily benefit you had selected. You may, though, come across indemnity or per diem plans. Such plans will pay you the full daily nursing-home benefit you chose, regardless of the actual charges, and you keep any surplus to spend as you wish. Expect to pay higher premiums for an indemnity plan.

Benefit period

This is the other factor that determines the total pool of money available for your care. For example, if you have a $150 daily benefit, a three-year policy will give you a lifetime benefit of $164,250 (365 days x 3 years x $150).

Insurance companies offer benefit periods that range from two years to lifetime (unlimited). The average stay in a nursing home, however, is 2.4 years. So you'll have to decide how close you want to stick to the average.

Waiver of premium

Waiver of premium should be part of your plan. This means that if you require care, you would not pay premiums after a set time of receiving such care. Also confirm that it applies to home care. Some policies only offer this rider for institutionalized care. Others require both a period of confinement and a period of time during which benefits have been paid.

Benefit reinstatement – lifetime maximum

Some policies will restore the number of days of coverage, dollar amounts available, or the maximum benefit, if you leave a nursing home and do not return within a certain period, for instance six months.

Options

There's a full menu of options available with most companies' products. It's kind of like trying to buy a new car. And insurers are constantly adding and revising options to meet consumers' needs. Some of the most common are the:

Inflation rider

With rising health care costs and the growing number of boomers impacting future demand, the expense of care will surely be much higher 30 years from now than it is today.

From 2004 to 2005, the daily cost for nursing homes and home health care aids rose over 5%. Yet the Consumer Price Index went up less than 3.5%. If this trend continues, a 55-year-old could see today's $203 average daily rate more than double to $422 by the time he or she is 70. That's $154,000 at year.

The inflation rider can help offset these increase by automatically boosting your daily benefit each year without a corresponding premium increase.

5% compound inflation rider

This allows your maximum daily benefit to increase by 5% each year for the life of the policy. For example, if you bought a $100 per day plan, after one year your benefit will be $105; in ten years, $162.89; in 20, $265. The compounded increase could be a valuable benefit for boomers who might not need to use their policy for many years.

re benefit

needed long-term care, where would you prefer to
?

a nursing home
an assisted living facility
your home

wer should be obvious. And many older people will agree.
es as many elderly people with disabilities live at home
an in a nursing home.[11]

olicies offer an option that will pay for home health care
ult day care. Some also allow care in assisted living
s. The available benefit can range from 25% to several
he daily nursing home benefit, depending on who provides
e. And although professional homecare providers will not
the type of care that friends and family can offer, they can
our love ones' task a lot easier.

sure that your policy's home care option includes coverage
stodial care, since that's what most people need. Also watch
r requirements stating that the care must be provided by an

omecare benefit can be used to pay for a variety of services
re not otherwise covered under the policy. These can help
remain in your home for as long as possible. Check out
care benefit riders that include:

Care planning visit
Home modifications

5% simple inflation rider

Your benefit would grow by a flat 5% annually. A $100 per day
benefit would increase to $105 after one year; to $110 in two
years; to $150 in ten years; and to $200 in 20.

Capped inflation protection

This starts out just like the compound inflation rider. But it will
only continue for a limited time, for instance 10 years. Thereafter,
the benefits will remain flat. Another type of cap may occur when
the policy's initial benefits have doubled.

This could save you money when compared to the compound
inflation rider. But consider this: Suppose you are 55. By the time
you are 70 and have a higher chance of needing special care, your
daily benefits will not go up for the rest of your life.

Note: If because of price concerns you have to choose between a
longer benefit period and the inflation rider, go with the inflation
rider. There's a greater chance that you'll need the inflation rider
than you would need a longer benefit payout.

Future purchase option

The FPO is a less expensive way to increase your daily benefit when compared to the inflation rider. It guarantees that you can increase the coverage in the future. Therefore, if a health problem sets in, you know that you can still buy more insurance to keep up with the daily rates in your community.

The problem is that when you do buy the additional coverage, the revised premium will be based on your age at that time—not how old you were when you originally bought the policy. Since the cost of insurance goes up as you get older, each daily benefit increase will cost more than the last one. And after you've exercised the FPO a few times, the premium might surpass what you would have paid with the inflation rider, which increases daily benefits without boosting the premiums.

Shared-care benefit policy

A shared-benefit policy gives married ⸱ to work with. For example, if you and y three-year policy with shared-care benefit⸱ care for one year, you or your spouse will benefits left. And in case one of you dies w benefits, the survivor will have access to the

Homeca

If yo receive i

A. In
B. In
C. In

The ans Six tim rather t

Most p and ac faciliti times the ca replac make

Make for cu out fo RN.

The that you hom

- Emergency medical response systems
- Durable medical equipment
- Caregiver training
- Home safety check
- Provider care check
- Elimination of waiting period
- Adult day care
- Hospice services
- Respite care (temporary overnight care)
- Double benefits for injury prior to age 65
- Pay for care provided by friends and family

Bed Reservation Benefit

What would happen if you were in a nursing home and had to temporarily go to a hospital? The nursing home could give your room to someone else. When you left the hospital there might not be any space available at that facility or any other in your community. Then you might have to go to a facility outside of your area, thereby making it difficult for friends and family to visit.

The bed reservation benefit insures that your space will be saved for you for a set number of days per year.

Return of Premium

Are you concerned that LTCI premiums will reduce the amount you'll leave to your heirs? The return of premium option will refund your premiums (less any benefits paid out) to your estate after you die. The policy might first require that you pay premiums for a certain number of years. Or it could have an age restriction, such as 70, after which the refund will not longer apply.

Nonforfeiture benefit

Some insurers will include this so that if you stop paying the premiums you remain eligible for at least a reduced level of the policy's benefits.

Travel coverage

Most policies will only pay benefits for long-term care provided within the U. S. This option will pay a benefit if you need assistance while traveling out of the country.

Survivorship benefit

If you and your spouse both own policies and one of you dies, the survivor won't have to pay any more premiums on his or her policy.

Other funding ideas

Besides taking the premium dollars right out of your pocket, there are some other ways to find the money to buy a long-term care insurance policy.

Immediate annuity

An immediate annuity is issued insurance company and will pay you an income for a preset number of years or your lifetime.

For example, suppose you are a 60-year old man and have $100,000 sitting in a low-return CD that you have no plans on using. You could take that money, purchase an immediate annuity, and receive $659 each month for the rest of your life.[12] The income from the annuity could be used to help pay the long-term care insurance premiums.

The same strategy could apply to the cash value from a life insurance policy that you no longer need. You would simply do a tax-free exchange into an immediate annuity to fund the LTCI payments.

Health savings account

Health Savings Accounts (HSAs) were created by the Medicare bill signed by President Bush on December 8, 2003 and are designed to help individuals save for future qualified medical and retiree health expenses.

You get a tax deduction for the amount you put in, the money grows tax-free, and there is no tax when you withdraw funds to pay qualified medical expenses. And long-term care premiums are considered one of the allowed expenses.

For more information on HSAs, visit the Department of The Treasury's Website listed in the Appendix.

FIND THE RIGHT COMBINATION

Even though price shouldn't be your only consideration, you may discover that you want the sports model with all the options, but you can't afford it. So you'll have to settle on the basic sedan.

It is important to make sure you can comfortably afford the LTCI. Otherwise, you might end up dropping the policy in a year or two. Then you're no better off—plus you're older and may have developed health problems that could make insurance more expensive or unobtainable.

And with all the choices, there is no reason for not coming up with a plan that meets your needs and price range.

Use the spreadsheet we've included as a way to compare several proposals. Once you've narrowed your selection to two companies, you might find that some of the options you want are included within the base price of one of the policies.

Here are some ideas for tradeoffs to consider if you find that the proposed premiums will zap your budget:

- You might reduce the yearly cost of protection by 35-to-40% by purchasing a three-year benefit vs. an unlimited benefit policy. It's better to have enough daily coverage with a shorter benefit period than a reduced benefit for a longer time. But is three years enough protection? A survey examined claims data from 1.6-million in-force policies. Only 14.4% of closed long-term care insurance claims lasted longer than 24 months (33.2% of open claims last longer than 24 months). The study further revealed that only 5.6 % of closed claims lasted longer than 36 months (16.2% for open claims).[13]

- Consider extending the waiting period.
- Look into shared-care benefit policies for you and your spouse. It'll be less than two individual policies with similar total benefit periods.
- Review your life insurance. Do you still need the coverage? The premium dollars might be better spent on LTCI if you no longer have as many dependents as you did when you bought the policy.
- You might find that the insurance company will give a discount if you and your spouse apply for policies at the same time. Depending on the company, this discount might also be available for unmarried cohabitants.
- Forgo options such as survivorship waiver of premium and cash benefits.

Prices vary depending on the policy and options you select. But to give you a bench mark, the American Association for Long-Term Care Insurance has put together this price index from their national study of average policy prices providing specified benefits.

- Age 55 - $772-per-year premium buys a $100 daily benefit with a three-year benefit period. Individual qualifies for preferred health and spousal discounts.
- Age 55 - $1,156-per-year premium buys a $150 daily benefit with a three-year benefit period. Individual qualifies for preferred health and spousal discounts.
- Age 65 - $1,456-per-year premium buys a $100 daily benefit with a three-year benefit period. Individual qualifies for standard health and spousal discounts.

- Age 65 - $3,068-per-year premium buys a $150 daily benefit with a three-year benefit period. Individual is single (standard health).

Note that inflation protection is *not* included in the above prices.

LIFE INSURANCE/LTC COMBINATION

Do you still need life insurance to provide for your survivors? Some companies offer a LTC rider for their life policies. Keep in mind, though, that the insurance company will check out your medical history quite thoroughly since they will be covering two risks: you needing LTC and dying. However, the premium might be lower than two separate life insurance and LTCI policies.

For example, a policy with a $250,000 death benefit might allow $10,000 per month withdrawals to pay long-term care expenses until the death benefit runs out. This way if you need long-term care, you collect. If not, your beneficiaries collect.

Second-to-die life insurance with the LTC rider could be another idea. As long as one of you is healthy, you stand a better chance of qualifying. And although this type of policy does not pay off until the death of the second person, it provides long-term care benefits to the surviving spouse.

Like anything else, though, there are advantages and disadvantages to owning long-term care coverage linked to your life insurance.

Advantages:

- Money that you have in the policy's cash value is available for non-LTC needs, such as a family emergency
- Your heirs are guaranteed an income-tax free benefit as long as no LTC benefits are used and/or no loans taken against the policy
- In case you require LTC, the money is available to pay for care in your home, a nursing home, an assisted living facility, or an adult day care center

Disadvantages:

- Money used for LTC will reduce the amount that passes to your survivors
- Does not allowed for shared benefits
- Does not offer martial discounts
- There is no tax deduction for the portion of the premium that applies to the LTC option, and it might actually be taxable since it is a distribution from the life policy

Make the company breakout the price for the LTC rider so you can compare it to a stand-alone policy. But remember: You're not getting two policies. Rather you're buying the option to choose how the benefits are paid out—while you are alive or after you die.

ESTATE PLANNING IDEA

Long-term care insurance can help reduce the estate tax bite for your heirs.

First, have an irrevocable life insurance trust (ILIT) purchase the LTCI. An ILIT, when structured properly, is not part of your estate and not subject to estate taxes.

Next, give money to your trustee each year to pay the insurance premiums. These gifts will reduce your taxable estate. The policy should include inflation-adjusted benefits and a return of premium rider. Then in case you need long-term care, pay the expenses out-of-pocket; thereby further reducing your taxable estate. The proceeds from the LTCI will go income and estate-tax free into the trust.

Finally when you die, 100% of the premiums that your trustee had paid for the LTCI will be refunded by the insurance company to the trust and bypass both income and estate taxes.

To make this concept work make sure the policy includes the following provisions:
- The contract must allow for a supplemental owner since the trust must own the policy.
- The daily benefits must be of an indemnity type so that the full amount is paid to the trust regardless of the actual charges incurred.
- The contract must include a return of premium rider. This means that the trust will receive 100% of the premiums paid after you die; no matter how much you may have used the policy's benefits.

As a hypothetical example, suppose that your estate tax rate is 50% (federal and state combined). If you had paid $400,000 in long-term care expenses, your estate would be reduced by that amount and thus save $200,000 in taxes. But your heirs would end up with $200,000 less ($400,000 spent minus $200,000 saved).

On the other hand, if you had a LTCI policy within an ILIT as outlined above, your estate would still save the $200,000 in taxes while your beneficiaries received the $400,000 in insurance benefits paid into the trust. Furthermore, the premiums that you had gifted to fund the LTCI will be returned to the trust and ultimately flow to your heirs.

	Without LTCI/ILIT	With LTCI/ILIT
Long-term care expenses	($400,000)	($400,000)
Estate reduction	$400,000	$400,000
Estate tax savings	$200,000	$200,000
LTCI benefits paid to ILIT		$400,000
Net benefits to heirs	($200,000)	$200,000

YOUR PREMIUMS MIGHT BE DEDUCTIBLE

Business owners can possibly deduct premiums their company pays. But that's not the only way to get a tax break. You can look into a tax-qualified policy.

But what in the world is a tax-qualified policy?

A tax-qualified policy offers certain federal income tax advantages in that if you itemize your deductions, you might be able to write off part of the premium.

But as with anything in the tax code, there's a catch—several in fact:

- Your premiums and your other deductible medical expenses must exceed 7.5% of your adjusted gross income before it will do you any good

- The IRS limits on the amount of LTCI premiums you can include in the calculation are based on your age:

    o Age 40 and under - $270
    o Age 41 to 50 - $510
    o Age 51 to 60 - $1,020
    o Age 61 to 70 - $2,720
    o Age 71 or over - $3,400

- The policy must meet special guidelines that you can read if you have trouble sleeping (See the link in the Appendix)

- The policy will only pay for federally-qualified expenses, thus it may be harder to get benefits. These qualified expenses must be for services and maintenance or personal care services that are required by a chronically ill individual pursuant to a plan prescribed by a licensed health care practitioner and include:

  - Diagnostic
  - Preventive
  - Therapeutic
  - Curing
  - Treating
  - Mitigating
  - Rehabilitative

Of course, the government has its own definition of a chronically ill individual.

For instance, you must be unable to perform without assistance from another individual a least 2 of 5 activities of daily living due to a loss of functional capacity (the ADL trigger) for 90 days.

This could mean a more restrictive policy. For example, suppose your tax-qualified policy includes 5 of the government's 6 ADLs (eating, toileting, transferring, bathing, dressing, and continence). And transferring (getting from your bed to a chair) is not one of them. You fall down, break your hip, and apply for benefits to pay an aid to help you get out bed.

Sorry—no benefits for you.

If you have your heart set on getting a deductible policy, you can read more about it on the IRS's Bulletin listed in the Appendix.

But the bottom line: To possibly save a few bucks in taxes, it might not be worth buying a policy that could severely restrict your benefits.

WAIT OR NOT TO WAIT?

LTCI premiums are age-and-health based. The older you are, the higher it costs. And if you aren't healthy when you finally do apply for coverage, companies might want a higher premium, exclude certain benefits, or refuse to insure you.

What is your family's health history? Even if you are healthy now, insurance companies will want to know how well your parents have done as they aged.

Long-term care can be especially devastating to boomers. For example, a person disabled at age 55 might need care for 30 years or more. Think it can't happen to you?

A study by Conning & Co. found that 40 percent of the people receiving care in this country are between the ages of 18 to 64.[14] But maybe you're healthy and never get sick. Great. Yet what would happen if you were permanently injured in a car wreck and needed care? How would you pay for it? Wait for the auto insurance companies and attorneys to fight it out? Good luck.

Still want to wait? Your chances of obtaining coverage could decrease with age.

A Wakely Actuarial Services' survey found that 10.7 percent of applicants between ages 50 and 59 who applied for long-term care insurance were declined coverage. And for individuals over 80 years old, 57.2 percent were not accepted.[15]

When should you buy coverage? Very simply put—at what age do you have assets to protect? If you are struggling to sock away money for retirement, you need to protect those dollars—now.

LTCI is part of the retirement package. For without it, your retirement is at risk.

And apparently people are starting to get the idea.

The average age of people buying LTCI has dropped from 72 in 1990 to almost 58.[16] Wonder why? Consider these points:

- Policies have improved over the past decade
- There are fewer alternatives available to pay for LTC
- Increased consumer awareness
- Changing family dynamics

But if you're still set on waiting, compare the rates for your current age to a person 10 years older. Although you'd save because you won't pay premiums for 10 years, the higher annual premiums in the future could wipe out those savings a few years thereafter.

You'll find that if you are healthy and in your 50s, the premiums can be considerably less than if you hold off until you are in your 60s. For instance a plan that costs a 55-year old $960 a year would cost a 65-year old $1940. Assuming each paid premiums until age 85; the 55-year old would spend $28,800, whereas the 65-year old would shell out $38,800. Plus if you wait, you take on the risk that your health could change for the worse, and you might not even qualify for the insurance.

In addition, according to a study by the American Association for Long-Term Care Insurance, individuals who are in good health might qualify for discounts that can possibly reduce the cost of long-term care insurance by 10% to 20% each year. The savings could amount to hundreds of dollars a year for a married couple.[17]

THE GOVERNMENT PUSHES FOR LTCI

The government has expanded its long-term care Partnership Program to all states. This program allows dollar-for-dollar Medicaid asset protection for individuals who buy tax-qualified long-term care coverage. Anyone who owns a partnership policy and applies for Medicaid can exclude assets equal to their total LTC coverage amount (up to $250,000) even after they have used up their insurance benefits.

Determine the amount of assets you want to shelter. For example, if you want to protect $150,000, you would buy a long-term policy that pays at least that amount in lifetime benefits. Then after your insurance runs out and you otherwise qualify for Medicaid, you get to keep $150,000 above Medicaid's limits.

The Program also stipulates that:
- Partnership policies will be treated the same as tax-qualified policies
- States can put the Program into place as soon as they get a Medicaid Plan Amendment approved
- The new provisions do not apply to existing policy owners, but participating states will likely allow exchanges
- The policies must include inflation protection:
    - Compound inflation protection for consumers age 60 and under
    - Some form of inflation protection for consumers ages 61 through 75

HOW TO JUSTIFY NOT BUYING LTCI

The following are excerpts from e-mails received after an article on long-term care insurance ran in an online publication.

Ralph M., 62, Provo, UT: *The premiums are so high, and you don't get anything tangible in return. I told my daughter that if she wanted to keep me from spending her inheritance and becoming a burden on her, then she could come up with the money.*

Well, Ralph, does your homeowners policy give you anything in return? How about your auto or health insurance? You get nothing unless something bad happens. So if your daughter does buy you a policy, I hope that you never do get anything in return.

****

Anne C., 51, Kansas City, KS: *I've put off buying a LTCI because the companies keep coming up with better benefits. I mean just a few years ago, home-care was just an option. Now all the companies are pushing it. And what if the whole health care system changes? My policy could be obsolete. Then I would have wasted all that money.*

Anne, you're right. Policies have change over the years—generally for the better. A policy you buy today will most likely have more benefits and fewer price increases than one you would have bought a few years back. However, policy premiums are age and health based. The longer you wait, the higher the price will be. And if your health changes, you might not even be able to buy one. If you're counting on the government to pick up the tab for boomers' LTC cost any time in the future—don't.

****

Carey H., 55, Des Moines, Iowa: *How do I know if the insurance company will be there when I might need them in 20 years? That would be terrible if I had spent all that money, and then the company went bankrupt. I couldn't afford a new policy, and I wouldn't have the money to pay for care myself.*

That's why it's important to make sure your company has high ratings with the major independent rating agencies. And check them out once a year. You can do it online or at the library.

****

Chuck D., 60, St. Petersburg, FL: *I think LTCI is a waste of money. Back when I was growing up, we took care of my grandparents when they got sick. And I helped take care of my parents, too. So I expect my kids to do the same. The government will pick up the tab if I need care the kids can't provide. I'll use my money for cruises, thank you.*

Works for me, Chuck. But think about this: Do you want to live in your child's house? Do they have a smelly, yappy dog that you can't stand? Do really think that you can put up with being around the grandchildren all the time? Most people would prefer to stay in their own home if their health changes. As far as the government helping you out, they'll only do that after you have spent all of your money. Meaning that if you get better, you'll have to be content to watch daytime TV instead of dancing the rumba in the Caribbean.

****

Harriet M., 69, August, GA: *My lawyer says I don't need insurance because Medicaid will pay for a good nursing home.*

Your lawyer may be right. But where will that nursing home be? And what about in-homecare? As the Federal deficit expands, Medicaid cut backs could mean less money for nursing home care. Consequently, Medicaid could pay for fewer nursing home beds in the future. And if you needed this type of care when no Medicaid-paid space is available in your community, you could be shipped off to someplace hours away from your friends and family.

****

Bart C., 78, Philadelphia, PA: *I'm a veteran. The VA will pay for my care.*

I'm all for helping vets, Bart. And as far as I'm concerned we don't do enough. But let's be practical—the facilities are government-run, and there's a waiting list to get in.

The VA doesn't give out long-term care benefits unless you:

- Have a 70% service-connected (SC) disability, or
- Are rated with a 60% SC and unemployable, or
- Are rated with a 60% SC and permanently and totally disabled

This tells me that if you are a vet without a severe service-connected disability, you won't get VA LTC benefits.

****

Gail A., 64, Dallas, TX: *I've heard that people who have $1.5 million or more don't need long-term care insurance.*

Congratulations for accumulating a nice net worth. Unfortunately, being a millionaire just ain't what it used to be.

You didn't get to be a millionaire by not thoroughly considering your options. So think about this: If you need nursing home care, a 2 ½ year stay will average $185,000 ($74,000 x 2.5). This average does not include any extras (i.e. medications, cable TV) you might need or want. Or maybe you'll want better than "average" care. That is a big chunk of change. Also the above figure is in today's dollars. Based on historical increases that 2 ½ year stay will cost you over $300,000 in 10 years. In 20 years the price could jump to almost $500,000. Multiply that possibly times two if you have a spouse.

Self-paying is the most expensive way to pay for care. You didn't do that to protect your home against a fire or other catastrophe, did you? For pennies on the dollar, you could transfer the risk of possibly needing LTC to an insurance company. Then you can keep most of your money to support the lifestyle you've become accustomed to and pass what's left to your love ones.

****

Cari E., 60, Miami, FL: *I don't need to worry about it. My family has a history of living long, healthy lives.*

On the contrary. You need to be concerned then about living a long life. If you became sick or injured, how will you pay for your care? Since you have good genes there's a high probability that you'll recover. If you spend a significant amount of your nest egg on long-term care expenses, what will be left to live on for the remainder of your life?

Long-term care insurance can meet that need.

****

Richard D., 59, Tempe, AZ: *I've received proposals from several insurance companies. Suppose that the insurance company I go with goes broke? Where does that leave me?*

If you've narrowed down your choice to two companies, pick the one with the highest credit rating. But in the unlikely event that it folds up, you at least can rest assured that all insurance companies that operate in your state are members of the state's Guaranty Association. This association was created to protect policyholders of an insolvent insurance company. The amount of protection varies among states. You can find your state's provisions at Website listed in the Appendix.

****

Bernie A., 55, Rochester, NY: *I'm sick and tired of paying for insurance. Car, disability, boat, health, life. It never stops. Why should I waste my money on more insurance premiums each month? I average about 7% a year on my investments. I think I'd be better off investing my money instead of spending it on premiums that I'll probably never get back.*

I feel your pain, Bernie. I hope you never do collect on your insurance benefits. Let's go over the numbers.

A plan that will pay $150 per day benefits for three years will cost you about $2,200 per year.[18] If you were to take that $2,200 each year and invest it for 10 years, assuming you continue to earn 7%, you'll have around $30,000 in your pocket. Not too shabby.

But suppose in 10 years you decide you better buy some long-term care insurance. Guess what? The premiums may be twice as much because you are 10 years older. And this higher rate could come at a time when you are retired and less able to afford the higher premium. In addition, suppose you are not insurable then? That $30,000 would pay for about 117 days (less than four months) of semi-private nursing care in Rochester at $257 per day.

Oops. I made a mistake. That's what the care would cost today. In 10 years, the rate could realistically be $419 day meaning you could only buy 72 days (2.4 months) of care.

Remember, Bernie, you have insurance to protect what you have. It's the mote that protects your financial castle.

AFTER YOU MAKE YOUR PLANS

Share your long-term care plan with your family. This applies whether you plan to self-insure, count on the government, or buy a long-term care insurance policy. What ever your choice, it will affect your family. They are the ones who will have to deal with filing claims and helping you get benefits. If they don't understand the process for meeting qualification periods, who can administer care, or what is covered, they'll become frustrated, and possibly miss out on getting you the benefits you deserve.

HYPOTHETICAL CASE STUDY

Fred is 58 years old, single, and healthy. His parents are in their 80's and in good health. Fred's agent gave him three LTCI proposals. We are going to walk him through the LTCI worksheet to watch Fred and his agent choose a policy.

Refer to the book's page number in the far right column in case you aren't sure about the information requested on the form.

		Company #1	Company #2	Company #3
Agency #1 rating	A.M. Best	B+	A	B++
Agency #2 rating	Weiss	C	B	B
Agency #3 rating	S&P	BBB	AA	AA
Avg. historical rate increases			7%	6%
Rate guarantee		years	N/A	N/A
To collect benefits, the policy requires				
	Certification of need		Y	Y
	Inability to perform number of ADLs		2	2
	Prior hospital stay		N	N
	Prior nursing home stay for home care		N	N
	Other		N	N
Definition of				

ADL				
	Eating		Y	Y
	Using the bathroom		Y	Y
	Moving from bed to chair		Y	Y
	Bathing		Y	Y
	Dressing		Y	Y
	Remaining continent		Y	Y
Pays benefits for mental illness & Alzheimer's?			Y	Y
Pays for care at any licensed facility?			Y	Y
If not, what are the restrictions?				
Wait period before benefits start				
	Nursing home	days	90-days	90-days
	Home care	days	0-days	90-days
How is wait period defined?				
	When impairment begins?			
	When qualified long-term care begins?			
	Continuous days of covered service		Y	Y
Daily benefit				
	Skilled care	$	$200	$200
	Intermediate care	$	$200	$200
	Custodial care	$	$200	$200
	Home care (hospice,	$	$200	$200

	respite, homemaker)			
	Adult day care	$	$200	$200
	Other (assisted living care)	$	$200	$200
Benefit type				
	Reimbursement		Y	Y
	Indemnity			
Max benefit period				
	Nursing home	years	3-years	3-years
	Home care	years	3-years	3-years
Waiver of premium				
	Nursing home		Y	Y
	Home care		Y	Y
Inflation rider				
	Compound annual increase	%	5%	5%
	Simple annual increase	%	%	%
	Capped inflation	years	years	years
If home benefits apply, what care is applicable?				
	Skilled care		Y	Y
	Care given by home health care aids		Y	Y
	Homemaker services		Y	Y
	Unlicensed relatives and friends		N	N
Home care benefit includes				
	Care planning visit		Y	Y
	Home modifications		Y	Y

	Emergency medical response systems		Y	Y
	Durable medical equipment		Y	Y
	Caregiver training		Y	Y
	Home safety check		Y	Y
	Provider care check		Y	Y
	Elimination of waiting period		Y	N
	Adult day care		Y	Y
	Hospice services		Y	Y
	Respite care		Y	Y
	Double benefits for injury prior to age 65		N	N
Max lifetime benefit				
	Nursing home	$	$219,000	$219,000
	Home care	$	$219,000	$219,000
	Total max lifetime benefit	$	$219,000	$219,000
Max out-of-pocket cost before benefits start				
(Local daily rate x wait period)	Nursing home	$	$18,000	$18,000
	Home care	$	$0	$18,000
	Adult day care	$	$0	$18,000
	Other	$	$	$
Waiting period for pre-existing conditions			N	N
Is the policy non-cancelable?			Y	Y

Tax qualified?			N	Y
Does the company check medical background?			Y	Y
Pricing				
Annual premium without any options		$	$ 1740	$ 1480
Inflation option - compound increase		$	$ 1650	$ 1230
Inflation option - simple increase		$	$	$
Home care option		$	$ 960	$ 0
Future purchase option		$	$	$
Shared-care option		$	$	$
Rate guarantee option		$	$	$
Bed reservation benefit		$	$	$
Nonforfeiture benefit		$	$ 522	$ 444
Return of premium benefit		$	$ 592	$ 503
Benefit reinstatement		$	$ 139	$ 118
International coverage		$	$	$
Waiver of premium	Nursing home	$	$ 0	$ 0
	Home care	$	$ 0	$ 0
Other options		$	$	$

Total of all selected options		$	$ 2610	$ 1230
Good health discount		$-	$-	$-
Is there a discount if you and your spouse buy?				
	Amount of discount	$-	$-	$-
Does the discount vanish when one spouse dies?				
Total annual premium with all options less discounts		$	$4350	$2710
Payment alternatives - base plan				
	Single pay premium	$	$	$
	10-year pay premium	$	$	$
	20-year pay premium	$	$	$
	Pay to age 65 premium	$	$	$

Let's go down each section.

Ratings

Each company received a Secure rating from A.M. Best. However, none of them were within our top two category requirement.

Weiss gave Company #2 and Company #3 a "B." This is their second highest category.

Finally, S&P gave companies #2 and #3 "AAs", their second highest category.

Company #1 did not receive ratings within the top two categories from any of the agencies. So we can cross that off the running.

Company #2 and Company #3 each received one of the top two ratings from Weiss and S&P. Therefore, both are still of interest.

Average historical rate increase

Company #2 has increased their rates an average of 7% and Company #3 increase theirs 6%. Both are reasonable. Neither offers a rate guarantee.

To collect benefits

Companies #2 and #3 both require a certificate of need and the inability to perform two ADLs.

Definition of ADL

Both companies use the same definition.

Pays benefits for mental illness and Alzheimer's

Both companies pay.

Pays for care at any licensed facility

Yes, for both companies.

Waiting period

Both companies have a 90-day wait before Fred could receive nursing home benefits. But note that Company #2 does not require any waiting period for home care benefits, whereas Company #3 has a 90-day requirement.

How is wait period defined

Both companies use the "continuous days of covered service" definition. This is the least preferable definition.

Daily benefits

Identical for both companies.

Benefit type

Both are reimbursement plans

Maximum benefit period

Both plans provide up to three years of benefits for nursing home and home care.

Waiver of premium

Both plans include this feature.

Inflation rider

Fred's agent suggested a 5% compound inflation rider, which is offered by both companies.

Care provided at home

Both companies will pay for similar services. Rarely will a company pay for care given by unlicensed relative or friends.

Home care benefit includes

Both companies offer similar features within their home care option, except for one. Company #3 does not eliminate the waiting period.

Maximum lifetime benefit

Since the maximum daily benefit and the maximum benefit period are the same for both companies, the maximum lifetime benefit is identical as well. $200/day x 365 days x 3 years = $219,000

Maximum out-of-pocket before benefits start

To keep it simple, we'll assume that the average rate of nursing home, home care, and adult day care in Fred's community is $200 per day.

With the 90-day waiting period, both policies would require that Fred shell out $18,000 before nursing home benefits begin.

Home care and adult care, though, is a different story. Using Company #2 he would not have to pay money before receiving benefits since the company does not have a waiting period for these services. However, Company #3's 90-day waiting period could cost Fred up to $18,000.

Waiting period for pre-existing conditions

Neither company requires this.

Is the policy non-cancelable

Neither company can cancel because of any changes in Fred's health after he buys the policy. Nor can they drop him because he uses benefits. The only way Fred's plan can terminate is if he decides to drop it or uses up his maximum lifetime benefits.

Tax qualified

Company #3's plan is tax qualified. Company #2's is not. Fred's income is low, and he doesn't itemize his deductions. Consequently, this is not important to him.

Does the company check medical background

Both companies will require Fred's doctors submit statements when he applies for coverage.

Pricing

Fred's agent offered several optional benefits. But Fred was concerned with rising prices. Plus he made it very clear that he wanted to be able to stay in his home to receive care if at all possible. For Company #2 these two options came to $2,610. However, you will see that Company #3's plan includes home care at no additional cost. Thus the only option Fred would have to pay extra for is the inflation protection at $1,230.

Payment alternatives

Since Fred's agent knew that Fred's money was tied up in several pieces of raw land and couldn't afford high premiums she did not propose any payment alternatives.

Conclusion

On the surface it may appear that Company #3's plan is a better deal. Heck who wouldn't want to spend $1,640 less a year on insurance premiums. For the most part it seems as good as Company #2's plan, and both are within Fred's budget. But recall two things about Fred. First, he is concerned about home care. He doesn't want to go to a nursing home unless he is so ill that there is no alternative. Second, Fred doesn't have any liquid investments he could quickly sell or the extra income to pay for care until his benefits kick in.

Company #3's plan has a 90-day waiting period on home care benefits. This means Fred would have to pay for his own care and come up with $18,000 for the first 90 days. This could be a problem for Fred.

Fred was willing to risk possibly needing $18,000 to cover a nursing home waiting period. And after going over the numbers, Fred and his agent decided that Company #2's plan was the better choice, even though the annual premium was more.

POLICY COMPARISON SPREADHEET

		Company #1	Company #2	Company #3
Agency #1 rating	A.M. Best			
Agency #2 rating	Weiss			
Agency #3 rating	S&P			
Avg. historical rate increases				
Rate guarantee				
To collect benefits, the policy requires				
	Certification of need			
	Inability to perform number of ADLs			
	Prior hospital stay			
	Prior nursing home stay for home care			
	Other			
Definition of ADL				
	Eating			
	Using the bathroom			
	Moving from bed to chair			
	Bathing			
	Dressing			
	Remaining continent			

Pays benefits for mental illness & Alzheimer's?				
Pays for care at any licensed facility?				
If not, what are the restrictions?				
Wait period before benefits start				
	Nursing home	days		
	Home care	days		
How is wait period defined?				
	When impairment begins?			
	When qualified long-term care begins?			
	Continuous days of covered service			
Daily benefit				
	Skilled care	$		
	Intermediate care	$		
	Custodial care	$		
	Home care (hospice, respite, homemaker)	$		
	Adult day care	$		
	Other (assisted living care)	$		
Benefit type				
	Reimbursement			
	Indemnity			
Max benefit period				

	Nursing home	years		
	Home care	years		
Waiver of premium				
	Nursing home			
	Home care			
Inflation rider				
	Compound annual increase	%		
	Simple annual increase	%		
	Capped inflation	years		
If home benefits apply, what care is applicable?				
	Skilled care			
	Care given by home health care aids			
	Homemaker services			
	Unlicensed relatives and friends			
Home care benefit includes				
	Care planning visit			
	Home modifications			
	Emergency medical response systems			
	Durable medical equipment			
	Caregiver training			
	Home safety check			
	Provider care			

	check			
	Elimination of waiting period			
	Adult day care			
	Hospice services			
	Respite care			
	Double benefits for injury prior to age 65			
Max lifetime benefit				
	Nursing home	$		
	Home care	$		
	Total max lifetime benefit	$		
Max out-of-pocket cost before benefits start				
(Local daily rate x wait period)	Nursing home	$		
	Home care	$		
	Adult day care	$		
	Other	$		
Waiting period for pre-existing conditions				
Is the policy non-cancelable?				
Tax qualified?				
Does the company check medical background?				
Pricing				
Annual premium without any		$		

options				
Inflation option - compound increase		$		
Inflation option - simple increase		$	$	$
Home care option		$		
Future purchase option		$	$	$
Shared-care option		$	$	$
Rate guarantee option		$	$	$
Bed reservation benefit		$	$	$
Nonforfeiture benefit		$		
Return of premium benefit		$		
Benefit reinstatement		$		
International coverage		$	$	$
Waiver of premium	Nursing home	$	$ 0	$ 0
	Home care	$	$ 0	$ 0
Other options		$	$	$
Total of all selected options		$		
Good health discount		$-	$-	$-
Is there a discount if you and your spouse buy?				
	Amount of discount	$-	$-	$-
Does the				

discount vanish when one spouse dies?				
Total annual premium with all options less discounts		$		
Payment alternatives - base plan				
	Single pay premium	$	$	$
	10-year pay premium	$	$	$
	20-year pay premium	$	$	$
	Pay to age 65 premium	$	$	$

APPENDIX

American Association for Long-Term Care Insurance:
http://www.aaltci.org

Daily long-term care rates:
http://www.metlife.com/WPSAssets/43838610601138293556V1F
2005NHHCSurvey.pdf

Department of The Treasury, health savings accounts:
http://www.treasury.gov/offices/public-affairs/hsa/

IRS Bulletin on tax-qualified policies: http://www.irs.gov/pub/irs-
irbs/irb97-21.pdf

Medicare's nursing home coverage and requirements:
http://www.medicare.gov/Publications/Pubs/pdf/10153.pdf

Medicaid's qualifications:
http://www.cms.hhs.gov/MedicaidEligibility/09_SpousalImpoveris
hment.asp

National Association of Insurance Commissioners:
http://www.naic.org/state_web_map.htm

National Reverse Mortgage Lenders Association
http://www.reversemortgage.org/

Nursing home and homecare costs:
http://www.metlife.com/WPSAssets/43838610601138293556V1F
2005NHHCSurvey.pdf

Ratings agencies

- A.M. Best: www.ambest.com

- Moody's: www.moodys.com

- Standard & Poors: www.standardandpoors.com

- Weiss: www.weissratings.com

State Guarantee Association:
http://www.nolhga.com/policyholderinfo/main.cfm/location/ga

State partnership programs:
- California: http://www.dhs.ca.gov/cpltc/
- Connecticut:
  http://www.opm.state.ct.us/pdpd4/ltc/Advisor/SaveMoney2
  006.pdf
- New York: http://www.nyspltc.org/
- Indiana: http://www.in.gov/fssa/iltcp/index.html

Tax-qualified long-term care insurance policy IRS guidelines:
http://www.irs.gov/pub/irs-pdf/p502.pdf

The Medicaid Planning Handbook by Alexander A. Bove, Jr.:
http://www.amazon.com/gp/product/0316103748/002-8859890-
8861632?v=glance&n=283155

INDEX

life insurance, 40, 43, 45, 47, 56
lifetime maximum, 31
look-back, 15
Medicaid, 4, 11, 13, 14, 15, 16, 17, 18, 54, 61, 83, 84
medical history, 45
medical investigating, 21
Medicare, 2, 11, 12, 17, 40, 83
MetLife Mature Market Institute, 3, 87
Moody's, 19, 84
non-cancelable, 69, 75, 80
Nonforfeiture benefit, 39, 70, 81
Northern Trust, 1
Options, 32
Partnership Program, 54
private nursing home, 3
rate guarantee, 22, 72
reimbursement, 29, 73
return of premium, 38, 47
reverse mortgage, 16, 17

S&P, 19, 20, 66, 72, 77
semi-private nursing home, 3
shared-benefit policy, 35
shared-care, 35, 43
skilled care, 11, 12
Social Security, 7, 17
Survivorship benefit, 39
tax deduction, 40, 46
taxable estate, 47
tax-deferred annuity, 56
tax-qualified policy, 49, 50
The Wall Street Journal, 4
Travel coverage, 39
trustee, 47
Urban Institute, 9
waiting period, 27, 37, 43, 69, 73, 74, 76, 80
Waiver of premium, 31, 68, 70, 73, 79, 81
Wakely Actuarial, 52
Weiss, 19, 20, 66, 71, 72, 77, 84
Women, 6, 87

¹

http://www.northerntrust.com/pws/jsp/display2.jsp?TYPE=interior
&XML=pages/nt/0605/1147987494825_694.xml
² http://www.johnhancock.com/about/news/news_jun2906.jsp
³ WSJ, 02/22/06, *Long-Term Planning: How to Protect Against the High Cost of Nursing Homes*
⁴

http://longtermcare.genworth.com/comweb/pdfs/long_term_care/A
LZ_finalreport_3-05.pdf
⁵ http://www.bls.gov/opub/cwc/tables/cm20050114ar01t3.htm
⁶

http://www.urban.org/UploadedPDF/311284_older_americans.pdf
⁷

http://www.cms.hhs.gov/MedicareProgramRatesStats/downloads/
MedicareMedicaidSummaries2005.pdf
⁸ http://www.ahca.org/news/nr050427.htm
⁹ 30Aug2006 www.aarp.org
¹⁰ MetLife Mature Market Institute, *Gender Differences: Do Men and Women View Long-Term Care Differently?*,
http://www.metlife.com/WPSAssets/86364650901100547914V1F
Gender%20Differences%20Report%20-%20Final.pdf
¹¹

http://www.urban.org/UploadedPDF/311284_older_americans.pdf
¹² Based on quotation dated 8/25/06 from
www.immediateannuities.com
¹³http://www.aaltci.org/subpages/media_room/story_pages/media0
91505.html
¹⁴ *Agent's Sales Journal*, 09/2005, *Long Term Care Insurance: Not Just for Seniors*

15

http://www.aaltci.org/subpages/media_room/story_pages/media03 0805.html

[16] Health Insurance Association of America

17

http://www.aaltci.org/subpages/media_room/story_pages/media02 2206.html

[18] Aug06, $150 nursing home and homecare daily benefit, three-year benefit period, 90-day elimination period, 5% compound inflation rider as offered by AARP.

Printed in the United States
76549LV00002BB/5

9 781601 450944